My First Riddle

Riddles From Across The UK & Overseas

Edited by Donna Samworth

First published in Great Britain in 2011 by:

Remus House
Coltsfoot Drive
Peterborough
PE2 9BF
Telephone: 01733 890066
Website: www.youngwriters.co.uk

All Rights Reserved
© Copyright Contributors 2011
SB ISBN 978-0-85739-367-8

Foreword

'My First Riddle' was a competition specifically designed for Key Stage 1 children. The simple, fun form of the riddle gives even the youngest and least confident writers the chance to become interested in poetry by giving them a framework within which to shape their ideas. As well as this it also allows older children to let their creativity flow as much as possible, encouraging the use of simile and descriptive language.

Given the young age of the entrants, we have tried to include as many poems as possible. We believe that seeing their work in print will inspire a love of reading and writing and give these young poets the confidence to develop their skills in the future.

Our defining aim at Young Writers is to foster the talent of the next generation of authors. We are proud to present this latest collection of anthologies and hope you agree that they are an excellent showcase of young writing talent.

Contents

Pierre Sowa (9) 1

Archbishop Wake CE Primary School, Blandford
Rosema Hossain (6) 1
Ethan Drewett (6) 2
Thomas Fuller (6) 2
Harry O'Loughlin (7) 3
Archie Miller (6) 3
Rowan Alice Haines (6) 4

Blessed William Davies Primary School, Llandudno
Emilia Farmanbar (6) 4
Chloe Hornsby (7) 5
Tamara Maund (6) 5
Brooke Hollis (7) 6
Ethan Piper (7) 6

Boskenwyn Community Primary School, Helston
Stephanie Nicholas (5) 7
Rufus Birkett (6) 7
Rossi Skingley (6) 8

Chacewater Community Primary School, Chacewater
Courtney Schmid (6) 8
William Ashurst (6) 9
Jasmine Kastoris (5) 9
Caleb Coventry (5) 10
Rhiannon Schmid (6) 10

Cornwood CE Primary School, Cornwood
Zara Penn (6) 11
Lucy Barnfield (6) 11
Emily Adams (6) 12
Myrtle Reedthomas (6) 12

Diptford CE Primary School, Totnes
Grace Morris (6) 13
Yana Botley (6) 13
Jacob Gillmore (6) 14
Katy Damerell (6) 14

Niamh Moore (6) 15
Shayma Abdul-Hamid (6) 15
Keziah Lyon (6) 16

Galley Hill Primary School & Nursery, Hemel Hempstead
Ellie Howard (6) 16
Lucie Simpson (6) 17
Sophie Smith (5) 17
Pelumi Adekunle (6) 18
Carlton Edwards (5) 18
Sonny Evans (7) 19
Lewis Hunt (7) 19
Aniekanabasi Enobong Inyang (6) 20
Tyler Lewis Channer (7) 20
Jasper Buckland (5) 21
Maddie Hooker (6) 21
Lucas Bennett (5) 22
Samuel Chapman (6) 22
Nojus Milkonas (6) 23

King's School, Mannamead
Edward Salisbury (6) 23

Linton Mead Primary School, Thamesmead
Meg Hanley (5) 24
Maryam Mohd Fauzi (6) 24
Alfie Hunter (5) 25
Bethany Higgins (5) 25
Rio Bolton (6) 26
Callum Ryan (5) 26
Amber Cowdrey (5) 27
Tiana Vutabworova (5) 27
Gare Oyoyo (5) 28
Elizabeth Jatto (5) 28
Sonia Bello (5) 29

Minehead First School, Minehead
Ellis Eglese (6) 29
Alicia Wood (6) 30
Amandine Woodberry (6) 30
Olivia Spiers (6) 31
Isabelle Norman (6) 31

Marli Robinson Pope (6)	32
Louis McCannon (6)	32
Mia Dover (7)	33
Tamzin Brown (6)	33
Jadan Hanson (6)	34
Sophie Haden (6)	34
Harry Reeder (6)	35
Alisha Yates (6)	35
Daisy-Grace Foster (6)	36
Paige Harding-Smith (6)	36
Ryan Chilcott (6)	37
Dellen Marshall (6)	37
Chloe Finch (6)	38
Brandon Williams (6)	38
Erin Treadaway (6)	39
Callum Dewar (6)	39
Alban Demiri (6)	40
Lovely-Joyce Follosco (6)	40
Jessica-Rae Fitt (6)	41
Erin Tremain (6)	41

Pimperne Primary School, Pimperne

William Dewar-Cutts (6)	42
Caroline Smith (7)	42
Grace Smurthwaite (6)	43
Jamie Sharp (6)	43
Ellie Dawes (6)	44
Isla Rose Howieson (6)	44
Harry Green (7)	45
Joshua O'Boyle (6)	45

Princess Frederica CE (VA) Primary School, Kensal Green

Eleanor Haines (9)	46
Zico Asare (10)	46
Jessica Spanier (9)	47
Ava Burch (7)	47
Mila Konwerska (8)	48
Ellie Moss (8)	48
Rebecca Christopher-Wait (7)	49
Ruby Chu (6)	49
Mattia Richardson (7)	50
Claudia Spanier (6)	50
Siân Baptiste (6)	51
Dylan Pascoe-Ericsson (6)	51

St Erme with Trispen CP School, Truro

Finley Holt (6)	52
Rebecca Mitchell (6)	52
Joshua Harbage (6)	53
Freya Booker (6)	53
Jeana Stephens (7)	54
Leon Langmaid (6)	54
Amy Trethewey (6)	55

St George's School, Germany

Till Ordemann (5)	55
Katy Jilbert (5)	56
Leo Hilgers (5)	56
Valentin Soulier (5)	57
Lilli Haas (5)	57
Charlotte Sommer (4)	58
Melaniya Evdokimova (6)	58
Kristian Hustrulid (6)	59
Victoria Drews (5)	59
Gregor Giesler (6)	60
Christopher Book (6)	60
Riccardo Eickvonder (6)	61
Kate Hazlehurst (5)	61
Maximilian Prill (6)	62
Quinn Friedrich (7)	62
Amelia Green (6)	63
Philip Leu (6)	63
Nicholas Puffer (6)	64
Samuel Thomas (6)	64
Vincent Kreutzer (6)	65
Mariella Clever (6)	65
Maxi Montag (6)	66
Kaan Erciyaz (6)	66
Chelsy Maxima Bunse (6)	67
Megan Herzberg (6)	67

St John's School, St John

Samuel Mundy (6)	68
Lola Gardiner (6)	68
Sinéad Duval (6)	69
Storm Dickson (7)	69
Harry Waters (6)	70
Molly Harper (6)	70
Isabel Vibert (7)	71
Sonny Beau Hanson (6)	71

St Mary's Catholic Primary School, Bodmin
Emma Thomas (6) 72
Alisha Beer (6).......................................72
Tamzin Hannah Slater (6) 73
Jessica Nelson (6).................................73
Phoebe Thomas (6) 74
Abigail Pearce (6) 74
Amy Levicki (6) 75
Poppy Singleton (6)..............................75
Declan Thomas (6)................................76
Georgia Bruce (6)..................................76
Alex Hall-Walsh (6) 77
Niall Harris (7).......................................77
Mya Barclay (6) 78
Tegan Rowe (6) 78

St Mary's CE Primary School, Writhlington
Daisy Church (5) 79
Aliyah Docherty (5) 79
Xavier Shipton (5).................................80
Alfie Padfield (6) 80
Aaron Carver (6)....................................81
Abi Bester (5)..81
Emmi Myers (5) 82
Gracie Padfield (5) 82
Lewis Harvey Davis (6).........................83
Liam Williams (6) 83

Sandford School, Sandford
Antek Wozny (6) 84
Ben Boughey (6) 84
Alice Board (7).......................................85

Sidbury CE Primary School, Sidbury
Lucy Spiller (6) 85
Luke Wheeler (6) 86
Maisie Lyon (6) 86
Holly White (6) 87
Sky Rowbotham (6)...............................87
Alice Chapman (7) 88
Oliver Beech (5)....................................88
William Bolton (5) 89
George Chapman (5) 89
Ben Green, Will Crick, Ben Fisher,
Sam Putman,Reuben Thomas (5)
& Dylan Green (6)................................90

Freddie Eul-Barker (7) 90
Jake White (6) 91
Eve Chinery (6) 91

Stoneydelph Primary School, Stoneydelph
Tayla Brazier 92
Pheobe Brown (6) 92
Corey Drew (6) 93
Caitlin Riley...93
Jessica Harris-Powell (6)......................94
Korey Fulton (5) 94
Quintana Jones 95
Megan Mellors......................................95
Dylan Dodwell (6) 96

Ysgol Bryn Coch, Mold
James Andrew Payton (7) 96
Callum Drew (6) 97
Melissa Hughes (7) 97
Josie Tattum (6) 98
Elliot Piers Lamb (6) 98
Jared Cresswell (6) 99
Harry Stinton (7) 99
James Edwards (6) 100
Poppy May Evans (6) 100
Adam Stowell (6) 101
Grace Mair Brockley (6) 101
Harry Crawshaw (7)............................102
Ella Blythin (6)....................................102
Katie Lenden (6)..................................103
Lauren Hannah Cox (6)......................103
Charlie Cooper (6) 104
Deran Hughes (6)................................104
Kaelum Hughes (6) 105
Oliver Cheatle (6) 105
Joel Eccles (6).....................................106

The Poems

My First Riddle –
RIDDLES FROM ACROSS THE UK & OVERSEAS

Theo

He's as fast as a world class gymnast,
He's as lovely as a rose,
He's as fast as a flash of light,
He's as quiet as a mouse,
His hair is as black as the night sky,
He's as brave as a lion,
He is as skilful as Maradona,
His team jersey is as red as blood,
He twists and turns like a slithering snake,
He is as young as a baby koala,
He's Theo Walcott, the Arsenal winger.

Pierre Sowa (9)

My Mum

She is as beautiful as a flower.
She is as famous as a rock star.
She is as sweet as a baby.
My mum.

Rosema Hossain (6)
Archbishop Wake CE Primary School, Blandford

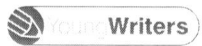

My Cat

He is as black as the engine.
He is as tiny as a mouse.
He jumps like a barmy horse.
He is my cat, Cheetah.

Ethan Drewett (6)
Archbishop Wake CE Primary School, Blandford

Captain Barnacles

He's as careful as a rocket driver.
Speedy as a car.
He's as quick as Superman.
He's Captain Barnacles.

Thomas Fuller (6)
Archbishop Wake CE Primary School, Blandford

My First Riddle -
RIDDLES FROM ACROSS THE UK & OVERSEAS

Football Star

He is as fast as a cheetah.
He is as grumpy as a rhino.
He is as strong as an elephant.
He skids like a frog.
He scores like a winner.
He is David Beckham.

Harry O'Loughlin (7)
Archbishop Wake CE Primary School, Blandford

Football Star

He runs as fast as a lion.
He plays football like a magic man.
He skids like a frog.
He scores like Robbie Keen.
He's . . .

Archie Miller (6)
Archbishop Wake CE Primary School, Blandford

My Sister

She is as funny as a clown
She is as rude as a monkey
She doesn't take much food
She is really loud at night
She doesn't go to sleep
She drops food on the floor
She is my sister Esme.

Rowan Alice Haines (6)
Archbishop Wake CE Primary School, Blandford

Untitled

It's as soft as a dog
It's better than a mouse
It's as cute as a cat
It's nicer than my dad
It's more gorgeous than my brother
It's a red squirrel.

Emilia Farmanbar (6)
Blessed William Davies Primary School, Llandudno

My First Riddle –
RIDDLES FROM ACROSS THE UK & OVERSEAS

Untitled

She's as clever as a dragon,
She's as lovely as a tiger,
She's as chatty as a parrot,
She's as pretty as a princess,
She's kinder than anyone,
She's Hailey Hornsby, my gorgeous sister.

Chloe Hornsby (7)
Blessed William Davies Primary School, Llandudno

Untitled

He's as fast as a cheetah,
He's a footballer,
He's as strong as a dog,
He's as kind as my dad,
He's as good as my friends,
He's as cool as a monkey,
He's the best footballer,
He's Steven Gerrard.

Tamara Maund (6)
Blessed William Davies Primary School, Llandudno

My Best Friend

He's as playful as a kitten,
He's stronger than my cousin,
He's furry as a rabbit,
He's white as snow,
He's Charlie, my pony.

Brooke Hollis (7)
Blessed William Davies Primary School, Llandudno

Untitled

He's as busy as a bee.
He's as clever as a professor.
He's as strong as the Hulk.
He's as funny as a clown.
He's as cool as Batman.
He's my dad.

Ethan Piper (7)
Blessed William Davies Primary School, Llandudno

My First Riddle –
RIDDLES FROM ACROSS THE UK & OVERSEAS

Mars

Spaceship rider
From far away.
Slimy, green skin,
Eyes on his hands.
Alien.

Stephanie Nicholas (5)
Boskenwyn Community Primary School, Helston

Sneaky Animal

Hairy, grey fur,
It kills.
It has sharp teeth,
It is mean.
It likes to eat dead animals
And sneaks around old grannies' cottages.
The wolf.

Rufus Birkett (6)
Boskenwyn Community Primary School, Helston

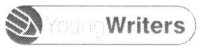

The Big Attack

It's like a steel person,
It deletes things,
It disappears too,
It's a terror for Amy Pond.
The Doctor tries to defeat it.
Cyberman.

Rossi Skingley (6)
Boskenwyn Community Primary School, Helston

Untitled

He is as funny as a monkey.
He is as happy as a horse.
He is as grumpy as a pop star.
He is as naughty as a dog.
He is very jumpy like a whale.
He is very sleepy like a person.

Courtney Schmid (6)
Chacewater Community Primary School, Chacewater

My First Riddle – RIDDLES FROM ACROSS THE UK & OVERSEAS

Messi

I love him the same as a dog.
He is cooler than a cat.
His hair is browner than a toad.
His tricks are better than a giraffe.
He is a better footballer than Rooney.
He is Messi.

William Ashurst (6)
Chacewater Community Primary School, Chacewater

Mum

She is as cheeky as a monkey
She is as funny as a penguin
She is as pretty as a horse
She is as happy as a cat
She is as shiny as a giraffe
She is my mum.

Jasmine Kastoris (5)
Chacewater Community Primary School, Chacewater

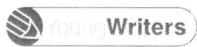

Dexter

He is clever.
He is as good as a hamster.
He is as fast as a cheetah.
He is my cat Dexter.

Caleb Coventry (5)
Chacewater Community Primary School, Chacewater

Rojos, The Rabbit

He is as clever as a wizard.
He is as fluffy as a cat.
He is as nice as a person.
He is as naughty as a secret.
He is as cheeky as a chipmunk.
He is as fun as a horse.
He is Rojos, the rabbit.

Rhiannon Schmid (6)
Chacewater Community Primary School, Chacewater

My First Riddle –
RIDDLES FROM ACROSS THE UK & OVERSEAS

My Teacher
(Dedicated to my granny)

My teacher's name is Claire
She is clever and very fair
She helps us at school to keep to the rules
There is no one to compare.

Zara Penn (6)
Cornwood CE Primary School, Cornwood

Twiggy

She is as pretty as a princess
She is as hungry as a lion
She is as fast as a cheetah
She is as gentle as a flower
She is Twiggy, my pony.

Lucy Barnfield (6)
Cornwood CE Primary School, Cornwood

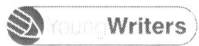

Kibble Fibble

She is as funny as a clown
She is as sad as a frown
She is as happy as a bird
She is as clever as a word
She is my sister Kibble Fibble, (Polly!)

Emily Adams (6)
Cornwood CE Primary School, Cornwood

Meat-Eater

He roars in anger.
He lies in the sun asleep
And flicks his tail.
He has sharp teeth.
He feels soft.
He's faster than a horse.
He's an orange and black tiger.

Myrtle Reedthomas (6)
Cornwood CE Primary School, Cornwood

My First Riddle –
RIDDLES FROM ACROSS THE UK & OVERSEAS

Who Is He?

He is as big as a rhino.
He is as funny as a monkey.
He is as kung fu loving as a kung fu master.
He is as noodle-loving as a Chinese man
He is as cake-loving as my dad.
He is Kung Fu Panda.

Grace Morris (6)
Diptford CE Primary School, Totnes

Who Is She?

She is as tiny as a gem.
She is as colourful as a rainbow.
She is as kind as an angel.
She is as beautiful as a flower.
She is as silent as a mouse.
She is as shimmery as a diamond.
She is a tooth fairy.

Yana Botley (6)
Diptford CE Primary School, Totnes

Who Is She?

She is as pretty as a butterfly.
She is as colourful as a rainbow.
She is as shiny as a star.
She is as good as a teacher.
She is as quiet as a mouse.
She is a tooth fairy.

Jacob Gillmore (6)
Diptford CE Primary School, Totnes

Who Is She?

She is as quiet as a mouse
She is as tiny as a rat
She is as colourful as a rainbow
She is as kind as an angel
She is as beautiful as a flower
She is as fluttery as a butterfly
She is as shiny as a star
She is as good as my mum
She is a tooth fairy.

Katy Damerell (6)
Diptford CE Primary School, Totnes

Who Is She?

She is as tiny as a gem.
She is as beautiful as a flower.
She is as colourful as a rainbow.
She is as quiet as a mouse.
She is as kind as a friend.
She is as hard-working as a farmer.
She is as shiny as a star.
She is the tooth fairy.

Niamh Moore (6)
Diptford CE Primary School, Totnes

Who Is She?

She is as tiny as a gem
She is as colourful as a rainbow
She is as kind as an angel
She is as fluttery as a butterfly
She is as beautiful as a crystal
She is the tooth fairy.

Shayma Abdul-Hamid (6)
Diptford CE Primary School, Totnes

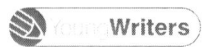 Writers

Who Is She?

She is as fluffy as a bear.
She is as black and white as a panda.
She is lovely.
She is as warm as a hot-water bottle.
She is as cuddly as a teddy.
She is as funny as a monkey chasing its tail.
She is as snuggly as a toy lion.
She is as beautiful as silver.
She is my cat.

Keziah Lyon (6)
Diptford CE Primary School, Totnes

The Spotty Riddle

I am spotty with black spots.
My ears are like a bear.
I sometimes hide in the grass.
My tail wags all the time.
What am I?
Dalmatian dog.

Ellie Howard (6)
Galley Hill Primary School & Nursery, Hemel Hempstead

My First Riddle -
RIDDLES FROM ACROSS THE UK & OVERSEAS

Wiggly Whiskers

I have fat legs.
My nose is wet.
I have paws.
I have wiggly whiskers.
I woof.
I wag my tail.
My bone I like.
I am a dog.

Lucie Simpson (6)
Galley Hill Primary School & Nursery, Hemel Hempstead

Untitled

I have black stripes.
I eat meat.
What am I?
A tiger.

Sophie Smith (5)
Galley Hill Primary School & Nursery, Hemel Hempstead

The Spottiest Riddle

I have sharp teeth.
My black spots are furry.
I like to eat meat.
My house is in Africa.
I can swim in the water.
What am I?
A leopard.

Pelumi Adekunle (6)
Galley Hill Primary School & Nursery, Hemel Hempstead

The Funny Riddle

I have wings.
My family can go underwater and so can I.
Me and my family live at the South Pole.
What am I?
A penguin.

Carlton Edwards (5)
Galley Hill Primary School & Nursery, Hemel Hempstead

My First Riddle –
RIDDLES FROM ACROSS THE UK & OVERSEAS

My Riddle

I only fly in the night because I'm invisible.
I drink cows' blood to stay alive.
My best friend is a superhero.
I live in a cave.
What am I?
A vampire bat.

Sonny Evans (7)
Galley Hill Primary School & Nursery, Hemel Hempstead

Untitled

I have a black and orange stripy tail.
I jump onto my prey when I eat my food.
My body has white, orange and black all over me.
What am I?
A tiger.

Lewis Hunt (7)
Galley Hill Primary School & Nursery, Hemel Hempstead

The Smelliest Riddle

I smell really bad
I am as stripy as a zebra
When people scare me I fart in their face
You can see me but can't hear me
What am I?
A skunk.

Aniekanabasi Enobong Inyang (6)
Galley Hill Primary School & Nursery, Hemel Hempstead

My Riddle

I am very fierce.
I eat meat and carry my babies by their neck.
I climb up trees.
What am I?
A lion.

Tyler Lewis Channer (7)
Galley Hill Primary School & Nursery, Hemel Hempstead

My First Riddle -
RIDDLES FROM ACROSS THE UK & OVERSEAS

Untitled

I have long claws
I run very fast
I eat buffalo
I live in the trees
I have black spots.
I am a leopard.

Jasper Buckland (5)
Galley Hill Primary School & Nursery, Hemel Hempstead

Untitled

I have colourful wings.
I like flowers.
I love to open my colourful wings.
What am I?
A butterfly.

Maddie Hooker (6)
Galley Hill Primary School & Nursery, Hemel Hempstead

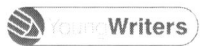

What Am I?

My favourite food is meat.
My fur is soft and I am yellow.
My claws are sharp.
I have a mane.
I live in the zoo.
I lick my paws.
What am I?
A lion.

Lucas Bennett (5)
Galley Hill Primary School & Nursery, Hemel Hempstead

Untitled

I have blue clear wings
And like to fly.
I have six black spots.
I like to eat leaves.
What am I?
A ladybird.

Samuel Chapman (6)
Galley Hill Primary School & Nursery, Hemel Hempstead

My First Riddle –
RIDDLES FROM ACROSS THE UK & OVERSEAS

Untitled

I can breathe underwater.
I have no legs.
You might find me at home.
What am I?
Fish.

Nojus Milkonas (6)
Galley Hill Primary School & Nursery, Hemel Hempstead

The Puma

He's a magnificent leaper like a frog.
He purrs like my cat.
He's wild like a lion.
He's unfriendly like a python.
He's rare like a dung beetle.
He's fast like a cheetah.
He's beautiful like a butterfly.
He's camouflaged like a red wolf.
He's black like space.
He is a puma.

Edward Salisbury (6)
King's School, Mannamead

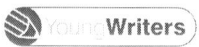

My Little Sister

She is as cute as a kitten,
She is as nice as a cat,
She is as beautiful as a flower,
She is my little sister Phoebe.

Meg Hanley (5)
Linton Mead Primary School, Thamesmead

My Mum

She is as lovely as a flower,
She is as nice as a cat,
She is as helpful as my friend,
She is my mum.

Maryam Mohd Fauzi (6)
Linton Mead Primary School, Thamesmead

My First Riddle -
RIDDLES FROM ACROSS THE UK & OVERSEAS

A Bug

He is soft
He is small
He is poisonous
He is red, green and orange
He is a bug.

Alfie Hunter (5)
Linton Mead Primary School, Thamesmead

My Cat

She is small,
She is friendly,
She is cute,
She licks everybody,
She is my cat.

Bethany Higgins (5)
Linton Mead Primary School, Thamesmead

Pet Dog

He is cuddly,
He is big,
He is nice,
He is special,
He is brown,
He is my pet dog.

Rio Bolton (6)
Linton Mead Primary School, Thamesmead

My Dog

She is so big,
She is lovely,
She has lovely hair,
She has a smooth body,
She is my dog.

Callum Ryan (5)
Linton Mead Primary School, Thamesmead

My First Riddle -
RIDDLES FROM ACROSS THE UK & OVERSEAS

My Mum

She is as good as a kid,
She is as pretty as a pony,
She is as nice as a flower,
She is as good as a mum,
She is as lazy as a lion,
She is my mum.

Amber Cowdrey (5)
Linton Mead Primary School, Thamesmead

My Brother

He is cheeky,
He eats my nose,
He is small,
He is Donovan, my brother.

Tiana Vutabwarova (5)
Linton Mead Primary School, Thamesmead

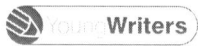

My Dad

He is special,
He is nice,
He is good,
He is kind,
He is my dad.

Gare Oyeye (5)
Linton Mead Primary School, Thamesmead

My Dog

She is big,
She is cute,
She is beautiful,
She has brown fur,
She is my dog.

Elizabeth Jatto (5)
Linton Mead Primary School, Thamesmead

My First Riddle –
RIDDLES FROM ACROSS THE UK & OVERSEAS

My Dad

He is as smart as my mum,
He is as clever as Meg,
He is as cool as Ben 10,
He is as big as Ross,
He likes to work,
He is my dad.

Sonia Bello (5)
Linton Mead Primary School, Thamesmead

What Is It?

It is smaller than a tiger.
It is rounder like a circle.
It can hop up in the air.
It can turn its head right round.
It's small.
It's a chicken.

Ellis Eglese (6)
Minehead First School, Minehead

What Is It?

It's as fluffy as a sheep,
It's as cuddly as a kitten,
It's as cute as a puppy,
It's as little as a mouse,
It's as fast as a horse,
It's as sweet as a chocolate cake,
It's as good as a show and puppets,
It's as nice as a shop,
It's as excellent as a regal theatre,
It's as rough as a cheetah and a lion,
It's as muddy as a pig,
It's as brilliant as a quad bike ride,
It is a bunny.

Alicia Wood (6)
Minehead First School, Minehead

What Is It?

It is as fierce as a dragon,
It is as yellow as the sun,
It is as smooth as a magic feather,
It is cuter than a kitten,
It is a lion.

Amandine Woodberry (6)
Minehead First School, Minehead

My First Riddle -
RIDDLES FROM ACROSS THE UK & OVERSEAS

What Is It?

It is the colour purple,
It is smooth and it is spongy,
It's jam and cream,
It is small,
It looks yummy and nice,
It is chocolate cake.

Olivia Spiers (6)
Minehead First School, Minehead

A Ladybird

It's as tiny as a bee and has black spots and red wings
It's little like a bee
It's as good as a puppy
It is so tiny
It's got four spots
It's got rosy-red wings
It's a ladybird!

Isabelle Norman (6)
Minehead First School, Minehead

Guess Who It Is

It's as cute as a pink flower,
It's as beautiful as a butterfly,
It's as funny as a clown,
It's as furry as a horse,
It's as nice as a Shetland pony,
It's as fluffy as a chick,
It's as sweet as a sweetie,
It's a rabbit.

Marli Robinson Pope (6)
Minehead First School, Minehead

What Are They?

I am as tall as a giraffe.
I can pick up heavy things.
I am as yellow as the sun.
I am as strong as a wrestler!
What am I?
I'm a crane.

I am as strong as a knight.
I'm as big as a castle.
I eat people.
I can smash houses.
What am I?
I'm a giant.

Louis McCannon (6)
Minehead First School, Minehead

My First Riddle – RIDDLES FROM ACROSS THE UK & OVERSEAS

What Is It?

It's as cute as a kitten,
It's as big as a flower,
It's as funny as a clown,
It's as slow as a train,
It's as brown as a horse,
It's as shiny as a hippo,
It makes wet noises,
It's as small as a pumpkin,
It's as big as a tooth,
It's as giant as a horse,
It's as fast as a cheetah,
It's as shiny as a pumpkin,
It's as cute as a baby tiger,
It's as small as an elephant,
It's as big as a mouse,
It's as smooth as a wall,
It's as hard as a leaf,
It's as smooth as a rock,
It's a cute little puppy.

Mia Dover (7)
Minehead First School, Minehead

What Is It?

It's hairier than a cat
It is better than watching TV
It is better than a cat
It is better than a cake
It's a dog.

Tamzin Brown (6)
Minehead First School, Minehead

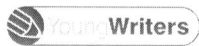

What Is It?

It is bolder than a man,
It is bigger than a bear,
It is as spotty as a dog,
Its shape is bigger than a dinosaur,
It's as big as a dragon,
It is as soft as a teddy,
It is as warm as a rabbit,
It is better than a bird,
It is a full stop.

Jadan Hanson (6)
Minehead First School, Minehead

Guess What It Is

It's as furry as a puppy,
It's as cute as a kitten,
It's as brown as a chocolate cake,
It's as fast as a cheetah,
It's as big as an elephant,
It's a pony.

Sophie Haden (6)
Minehead First School, Minehead

My First Riddle -
RIDDLES FROM ACROSS THE UK & OVERSEAS

Cheetah

It is faster than a champion runner,
It is faster than anyone,
It is an animal,
It is almost faster than a black leopard,
He has yellow and black spots,
It's faster than an Olympic runner,
It's smaller than an elephant,
It is faster than a person,
It is a cheetah!

Harry Reeder (6)
Minehead First School, Minehead

What Is It?

It's as soft as fur,
It's as cute as a puppy,
It's as little as a puppet,
It's as fast as a dog,
It's as good as a show,
It's a kitten.

Alisha Yates (6)
Minehead First School, Minehead

What Is It?

It is as spotty as a Dalmatian.
Its neck is as long as an elephant's trunk.
Its legs are as tall as a tree.
Its tail is as fluffy as a lion's mane.
It's a giraffe.

Daisy-Grace Foster (6)
Minehead First School, Minehead

It Is . . .

It is as big as a horse.
It is as long as a giraffe.
It is grey like a guinea pig.
Its ears are as big as the world.
It is an elephant.

Paige Harding-Smith (6)
Minehead First School, Minehead

What Is It?

It is as small as a puppy
Its tail is as long as an elephant's tail
Its whiskers are like a lion's whiskers
It is a cat.

Ryan Chilcott (6)
Minehead First School, Minehead

What Is It?

It is as spotty as a child with chickenpox,
It is as fast as a lion,
It is as orange as an autumn leaf,
Its tail is as long as Erin's plait,
It is a cheetah.

Dellen Marshall (6)
Minehead First School, Minehead

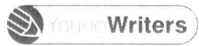

Untitled

Its hooves are as clip-cloppy as a horse,
It is as gallopy as a child jumping,
It is as soft as a lion's mane,
It is as cute as an ant,
It is as pretty as a princess,
Its horn is as pink and sparkly as a princess' dress,
It is a unicorn.

Chloe Finch (6)
Minehead First School, Minehead

What Is It?

It is as fat as a pig.
It is as big as a bear.
It is as slow as a snake.
It is an elephant.

Brandon Williams (6)
Minehead First School, Minehead

What Is It?

Its legs are as long as a donkey's leg
It is as brown as a pig
It is as big as a giraffe
Its tail is as long as my plait
When it walks it goes clip-clop
It is a horse.

Erin Treadaway (6)
Minehead First School, Minehead

What Is It?

It is as yellow as a lion's fur,
Its neck is as long as eight trumpets,
Its tail is as big as 11 people,
Its legs are as long as 2,000 people,
It's a giraffe.

Callum Dewar (6)
Minehead First School, Minehead

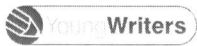

What Is It?

It is as prickly as a dinosaur's tooth.
It is as brown as a grizzly bear.
It is as fast as a snake.
It is a hedgehog.

Alban Demiri (6)
Minehead First School, Minehead

What Is It?

It is as pink as a cherry,
It lives at a waterhole like a hippo,
Its feathers are as soft as a pillow,
Its beak is as sharp as a needle,
It is a flamingo.

Lovely-Joyce Follosco (6)
Minehead First School, Minehead

My First Riddle -
RIDDLES FROM ACROSS THE UK & OVERSEAS

What Is It?

Its mane is as swishy as a tail.
Its gallop is as loud as a car's engine.
Its body is as big as a trampoline.
It is a horse.

Jessica-Rae Fitt (6)
Minehead First School, Minehead

What Is It?

It is as brown as a tree.
Its tail is as fast as grass.
It is a squirrel.

Erin Tremain (6)
Minehead First School, Minehead

Gorilla

He is as shy as a monkey,
He is as strong as a wrestler,
He is as big as a giant,
He is as cool as a guitar,
He is a gorilla.

William Dewar-Cutts (6)
Pimperne Primary School, Pimperne

The Wonderful Adventure

It's as little as a mouse,
It's as precious as money,
It's as bright as the sun,
It's as colourful as a rainbow,
It's a gem.

Caroline Smith (7)
Pimperne Primary School, Pimperne

My First Riddle -
RIDDLES FROM ACROSS THE UK & OVERSEAS

The Sweet Poem

She is as sweet as a bird,
She is as clever as a scientist,
She is as sweet as a flower,
She has long hair,
She is Caroline.

Grace Smurthwaite (6)
Pimperne Primary School, Pimperne

Untitled

It is as fierce as a shark,
It is as hoppy as a kangaroo,
It has as good hearing as a cat,
It is a rabbit!

Jamie Sharp (6)
Pimperne Primary School, Pimperne

Dogs

She is as clever as an acrobat.
She is as clever as a fluffy thing.
She is as clever as an artist.
She is as lovely as a kitten.
She is as beautiful as a feather.
She is a dog.

Ellie Dawes (6)
Pimperne Primary School, Pimperne

Cool

She's as cool as a rock star,
She's as wonderful as an angel,
She's as pretty as a ballerina,
She's as clever as an elephant,
She's Cheryl Cole.

Isla Rose Howieson (6)
Pimperne Primary School, Pimperne

My First Riddle -
RIDDLES FROM ACROSS THE UK & OVERSEAS

Tiger Tank

It's as strong as a leopard,
It's as big as an elephant,
It's as powerful as a lorry,
It's as chunky as a hill,
It's a Tiger Tank.

Harry Green (7)
Pimperne Primary School, Pimperne

It's Not A Chicken

It's as white as a dog
It's as jumpy as a kangaroo
It's as fast as a ostrich
It's as hungry as a guinea pig
It's a rabbit.

Joshua O'Boyle (6)
Pimperne Primary School, Pimperne

Untitled

She's as noisy as an elephant,
She's as cool as a cucumber,
She's as pretty as a rose,
She's as fiery as the sea storm,
She's as quick as a motorbike,
She's as adventurous as an explorer,
She is Sam Boat, the girl next door.

Eleanor Haines (9)
Princess Frederica CE (VA) Primary School, Kensal Green

Untitled

As red as strawberries,
They're as quick as the speed of light,
As strong as a bull,
They're as brave as a lion,
Their speed is the same as a cheetah,
They multiply quickly as a swarm of bees,
They are called Arsenal.

Zico Asare (10)
Princess Frederica CE (VA) Primary School, Kensal Green

My First Riddle –
RIDDLES FROM ACROSS THE UK & OVERSEAS

Untitled

You celebrate it once a year,
You get lots of presents if you're lucky,
You sing a special song,
You eat sweet things and treats,
Your family and friends might come over,
You would probably have a party each time you get older.
It's my birthday.

Jessica Spanier (9)
Princess Frederica CE (VA) Primary School, Kensal Green

My Dad

He's as strong as a tiger,
He's as brave as a lion,
He's as handsome as a prince,
He's as tall as a giraffe,
He's as cuddly as a kitten,
He's as fun as a funfair ride,
He's as kind as your best friend,
He's as faithful as a dog,
He's as funny as a clown,
He's as wise as an owl,
He's as cheerful as a sunny day,
He's my dad.

Ava Burch (7)
Princess Frederica CE (VA) Primary School, Kensal Green

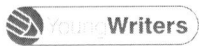

Untitled

She is as funny as an excited puppy,
She's as cheeky as a monkey,
She's as cute as a rosebush,
She sings like a robin,
She eats like a royal,
She dances like someone from 'Come Dancing',
She is as beautiful as the universe,
She is as funny as a comedian,
She sparkles like a crystal,
She is my friend, Lily Garnett.

Mila Konwerska (8)
Princess Frederica CE (VA) Primary School, Kensal Green

Cute Little Phoebe

She's as cute as a button,
She's as cheeky as a monkey,
She's as curly as a Curly Wurly chocolate bar,
She's as chubby as a pillow when it is puffed up,
She's got eyes as blue as the sea,
Her hair is as gold as the sun,
Her cheeks are as rosy as the rosiest rose,
She's Phoebe, my sister.

Ellie Moss (8)
Princess Frederica CE (VA) Primary School, Kensal Green

Untitled

She is as cool as a rock band,
She's as cute as my little kitten,
She is as fast as a cheetah,
She's as fun as a rocking chair,
She's as bright as the sun,
She's as clever as a teacher,
She's as amazing as the stars,
She's my cousin, Courtney.

Rebecca Christopher-Wait (7)
Princess Frederica CE (VA) Primary School, Kensal Green

Untitled

He's as fast as a cheetah,
He's as funny as a clown,
He's as soft as a blanket,
He's as friendly as Father Christmas,
He's as silly as a monkey,
He is Harley the dog.

Ruby Chu (6)
Princess Frederica CE (VA) Primary School, Kensal Green

Someone I Love

She's as plump as a pumpkin,
She's as funny as a clown,
She's as curious as a meerkat,
She's as sweet as a lolly,
She's as pretty as a doll,
She's as bossy as a team captain,
She's Sophia, my sister.

Mattia Richardson (7)
Princess Frederica CE (VA) Primary School, Kensal Green

Untitled

She is cool as a rock star,
She is loud as a roaring lion,
She is as beautiful as a sunrise,
She is like the sweetest tulip in a bunch of flowers,
Her cooking makes my tummy fizz,
She is as brave as a knight,
She is as clever as me,
She is my mum.

Claudia Spanier (6)
Princess Frederica CE (VA) Primary School, Kensal Green

My First Riddle - RIDDLES FROM ACROSS THE UK & OVERSEAS

Untitled

She's as funny as a clown,
She's as good as my mum,
She's as happy as my dad,
She's as troublesome as my brother,
She's as helpful as Mother Theresa,
She is my mum.

Siân Baptiste (6)
Princess Frederica CE (VA) Primary School, Kensal Green

Untitled

He is as brown as a conker,
He is soft like a marshmallow,
He is as furry as a bear,
He is special like my birthday,
He is Harry, my cuddly toy.

Dylan Pascoe-Ericsson (6)
Princess Frederica CE (VA) Primary School, Kensal Green

What Am I?

I have eyes and blue antennae.
I have shiny patterns.
I have pretty wings.
I drink nectar.
Butterfly.

Finley Holt (6)
St Erme with Trispen CP School, Truro

Who Am I?

I am a fast runner, very fast indeed.
Nobody can catch me.
I need food to eat.
I gulp like a fast disco ball.
I am very big and tall.
Who am I?

Rebecca Mitchell (6)
St Erme with Trispen CP School, Truro

My First Riddle -
RIDDLES FROM ACROSS THE UK & OVERSEAS

What Am I?

I am beautiful and shiny like a fluttery feather,
I can fly gracefully among the sky,
When it's a sunny day I lay eggs for my babies,
If you come near me I will flutter away
And if you're lucky I might stay where I am,
What am I?
Butterfly.

Joshua Harbage (6)
St Erme with Trispen CP School, Truro

What Am I?

I am horrible just like a lion.
I have a humongous black body.
I have big, long, pointy legs.
I can run very, very fast like a cheetah.
I can bite if you scare me away.
I can quickly catch bugs in my web.
What am I?
Tarantula.

Freya Booker (6)
St Erme with Trispen CP School, Truro

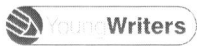

What Am I?

I have a tiny tail to carefully twitch.
My fur is as small as a spiky caterpillar.
Somehow I hate being picked tightly.
However I love delicious apples and carrots.
I'm wicked and I'm also very kind.
Proudly I bounce but not very high.
What am I?
Rabbit.

Jeana Stephens (7)
St Erme with Trispen CP School, Truro

What Am I?

I have two wings.
I fly as high as the clouds.
You sometimes see me in the grass.
If you go near me I will go after you.
I sometimes scare you.
I have two delicate wings.
You might see my shiny yellow and black stripes on me.
When I sting you it will hurt!
What am I?
Bumblebee.

Leon Langmaid (6)
St Erme with Trispen CP School, Truro

My First Riddle - RIDDLES FROM ACROSS THE UK & OVERSEAS

What Am I?

I'm as beautiful as a princess.
When I open my wings I start to flutter.
I fly in the blue sky gracefully.
I drink from a flower.
I started like a caterpillar.
What am I?
Butterfly.

Amy Trethewey (6)
St Erme with Trispen CP School, Truro

I Am A Shark

I am scary.
I have white teeth.
I have a fin on my back.
I am grey.
I eat fish.
I can swim.
What am I?
A shark.

Till Ordemann (5)
St George's School, Germany

My Riddle

I am very small.
I am red.
I have black spots.
I can fly.
I live in the garden.
I have eight legs.
What am I?
A ladybird.

Katy Jilbert (5)
St George's School, Germany

It Is A Zebra

I have black and white stripes.
I have four legs.
I have hooves.
I eat grass.
What am I?
A zebra.

Leo Hilgers (5)
St George's School, Germany

My First Riddle –
RIDDLES FROM ACROSS THE UK & OVERSEAS

What Am I?

I eat fish.
I am green.
I live in the river.
I have sharp teeth.
What am I?
A crocodile.

Valentin Soulier (5)
St George's School, Germany

Guess What I Am

I live in Antarctica.
I have two legs.
I like fish.
I like to slide over the ice.
I am a good swimmer.
I am black and white.
What am I?
I am a penguin.

Lilli Haas (5)
St George's School, Germany

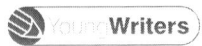

A Bumblebee

I am very small.
I am yellow.
I have black stripes.
I will sting you.
I say buzz, buzz!
I make honey.
What am I?
A bumblebee.

Charlotte Sommer (4)
St George's School, Germany

Autumn

It is as scary as a ghost.
It is as stormy as a rocket.
It is as cloudy as an aeroplane.
It is autumn.

Melaniya Evdokimova (6)
St George's School, Germany

Autumn

It is as scary as a ghost.
It is as scary as a witch.
It is as loud as a rocket.
It is as scary as a bear.
It is autumn.

Kristian Hustrulid (6)
St George's School, Germany

Who Am I?

I am a girl.
I have brown hair.
I have brown eyes.
I am called Victoria.

Victoria Drews (5)
St George's School, Germany

Who Am I?

I am a boy.
I have a pullover.
I have some blond hairs
And some brown hairs.
I have black boy shoes.
I am Gregor.

Gregor Giesler (6)
St George's School, Germany

What Am I?

I like to swim in the water.
I eat meat.
I live in Asia.
I live to run.
I catch animals.
I have no enemies.
I have black and orange stripes.
I have fur.
What am I?
(Tiger.)

Christopher Book (6)
St George's School, Germany

My First Riddle –
RIDDLES FROM ACROSS THE UK & OVERSEAS

What Am I?

I have a good nose.
I am a pet.
I have a brain.
I chase cats.
I have four legs.
I have puppies.
I am brown.
What am I?
Dog.

Riccardo Eickvonder (6)
St George's School, Germany

What Am I?

I have a very soft tail
I like nuts
I climb up trees
I chase animals round trees
I can run fast
I am brown
I run fast because I am scared
I have legs but I run on my hands
What am I?
Squirrel.

Kate Hazlehurst (5)
St George's School, Germany

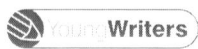

What Am I?

I have eight legs.
I eat my own babies.
I eat leaves too.
I spin webs.
I have different shapes.
I have very small eyes.
I have a small mouth too.
What am I?
Spider.

Maximilian Prill (6)
St George's School, Germany

Nicholas

He is my best friend,
He has dark skin,
He has dark brown hair,
I play with him a lot,
He is really nice,
He is Nicholas.

Quinn Friedrich (7)
St George's School, Germany

My First Riddle – RIDDLES FROM ACROSS THE UK & OVERSEAS

Sophia

She comes from Glasgow,
She is funny and has lots of silly bands,
Her brother has curly hair,
She loves drawing,
She loves sweets,
She is my friend Sophia.

Amelia Green (6)
St George's School, Germany

My Dog

He is brown,
He is very cool,
He likes us,
He is nice,
He can jump really high,
He is my dog.

Philip Leu (6)
St George's School, Germany

Quinn

He is as funny as a monkey.
He is as clever as a computer.
He is as cool as a motorbike racer.
He is as nice as pasta.
He is my friend Quinn.

Nicholas Puffer (6)
St George's School, Germany

Who Am I?

I am a boy.
I have brown eyes.
I have a pullover.
I have some shoes.
I have brown hair.
I am Oscar.

Samuel Thomas (6)
St George's School, Germany

My First Riddle –
RIDDLES FROM ACROSS THE UK & OVERSEAS

Who Am I?

She is small like a hedgehog.
She likes to cuddle like a bear.
She is nice like the sun.
She is laughing like a monkey.
She likes to eat ice cream like me.
She is my sister Frieda.

Vincent Kreutzer (6)
St George's School, Germany

Who Am I?

He is strong like a car.
He can run like a cheetah.
He is clever like a wizard.
He is funny like a clown.
He is scary like a vampire.
He is nice like a rainbow.
He is my brother Alex.

Mariella Clever (6)
St George's School, Germany

Who Am I?

She is as nice as a rainbow.
She is as cuddly as a dog.
She is as big as a mountain.
She is as funny as a clown.
She is as fast as a cheetah.
She is as clever as a teacher.
She is as tall as a horse.
She is as sweet as chocolate.
She is my sister Kristina.

Maxi Montag (6)
St George's School, Germany

Who Am I?

He is strong like a galaxy.
He is clever like me!
He is 41 years old.
He is tall like a mountain.
He is funny like a comedian.
He is my dad Oktay.

Kaan Erciyaz (6)
St George's School, Germany

My First Riddle -
RIDDLES FROM ACROSS THE UK & OVERSEAS

Who Is She?

She is white like snow.
She is soft like a cushion.
She likes to cuddle like a baby.
She is funny like a clown.
She is sweet like strawberry jam.
She is clever like a clever cat.
She is my dog Lines.

Chelsy Maxima Bunse (6)
St George's School, Germany

Who Am I?

He is dark like the night.
He is soft like a cushion.
He is funny like a clown.
He is fast like a cheetah.
He is clever like the clever cat.
He is sweet like strawberry jam.
He wants to eat very much like a lion.
He is my dog and he is called Paul.

Megan Herzberg (6)
St George's School, Germany

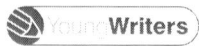

My Friend

He is as funny as a clown.
He is as slow as a gorilla.
He is as silly as my dad.
He is full of fun like a dog.
He is as nice as my best friend.
He is Finlay.

Samuel Mundy (6)
St John's School, St John

Untitled

He is as trusted as the Queen.
He is as happy as a dolphin.
He is as determined as an artist.
He is as smart as a judge.
He is as kind as my best friend.
His writing is as neat as the people who make menus.
He is Roald Dahl.

Lola Gardiner (6)
St John's School, St John

Untitled

She is as friendly as my best friend.
She is as helpful as a cat.
She is as polite as a doctor.
She is as quiet as a slug.
She is as cute as a cat.
She is Lara.

Sinéad Duval (6)
St John's School, St John

Untitled

He is as cool as my dad.
He is as happy as my dog.
He is as clever as my mum.
He is as brave as my sister.
He is as good a listener as my Lola.
He is as nice as my dog.
He is Hong Kong Phooey.

Storm Dickson (7)
St John's School, St John

My Friend Conor

He is as clever as a clown.
He is as kind as my mum.
He is as nice as my dad.
He is as friendly as my best friend.
He is as good as a singer.
He is as helpful as a dad.
He is Conor.

Harry Waters (6)
St John's School, St John

Rock Star

She is as kind as my mum.
She is smart like my dad.
She is musical like an instrument.
She is rocky like a star.
She is clever like my pet.
She is shiny like a diamond.
She is Hannah Montana.

Molly Harper (6)
St John's School, St John

My First Riddle – RIDDLES FROM ACROSS THE UK & OVERSEAS

Who Is He . . . ?

He is as clever as a star.
He is as kind as a dog.
He is as happy as my friend.
He is as smart as my mum.
He is an artist like Mrs Muir.
He is good at drawing cats.
He is Daniel Patrick Kessler.

Isabel Vibert (7)
St John's School, St John

Untitled

He is as popular as Elvis.
He is as cool as a wave.
He is as imaginative as a scientist.
He is as musical as my dad.
He is as smart as my mum.
He is as friendly as a cat.
He is Michael Jackson.

Sonny Beau Hanson (6)
St John's School, St John

A Riddle About A Platypus

I live in Australia.
I live outside.
I have a big black beak.
I have a fluffy body.
What am I?

Emma Thomas (6)
St Mary's Catholic Primary School, Bodmin

A Riddle About A Dog

I'm found at a pet store
I'm sometimes long, small, short or tall
I have sharp teeth
I have four legs and I'm furry
I can be black or white or brown or grey
I've got spiky whiskers
I have a black, wet nose
What am I?

Alisha Beer (6)
St Mary's Catholic Primary School, Bodmin

My First Riddle -
RIDDLES FROM ACROSS THE UK & OVERSEAS

A Riddle About A Zebra

I live in the wild and in a zoo.
I hide under trees when it's raining.
I gallop fast.
I have black and white stripes.
What am I?

Tamzin Hannah Slater (6)
St Mary's Catholic Primary School, Bodmin

A Riddle About A Squirrel

I scatter quickly
I live in the trees
I live in a drey
I love to climb trees
I can be red or grey
I live in the trees
I have a bushy tail
I eat nuts
What am I?

Jessica Nelson (6)
St Mary's Catholic Primary School, Bodmin

A Riddle About A Squirrel

I have two legs and two hands
I have triangle ears
I am brown
I live in a tree
I have bright eyes
I am soft
I have a bushy tail
I am fat
What am I?

Phoebe Thomas (6)
St Mary's Catholic Primary School, Bodmin

A Riddle About A Lion

I live in Africa.
I am a very good swimmer.
I hunt if I am a female.
I have sharp teeth.
I am yellow.
What am I?

Abigail Pearce (6)
St Mary's Catholic Primary School, Bodmin

A Riddle About A Blue Whale

I am a mammal.
I have brushes by my mouth.
I have a hole in my back.
I am the biggest animal in the world.
I am grey and I swallow fish.
What am I?

Amy Levicki (6)
St Mary's Catholic Primary School, Bodmin

A Riddle About A Rabbit

I can live indoors and outdoors
Sometimes I can be grey or white
I have a fluffy, round tail
I have fluffy, tall ears
I love to eat carrots
What am I?

Poppy Singleton (6)
St Mary's Catholic Primary School, Bodmin

A Riddle About A Leopard

I am taller than a table.
I live in the wild but you can see me in the zoo.
I use my sharp claws to help me climb.
People kill me for my spotty skin.
I have a long tail
And I hunt for food.
What am I?

Declan Thomas (6)
St Mary's Catholic Primary School, Bodmin

A Riddle About A Cat

I can be furry.
You can get me from the pet shop.
I am soft.
I have whiskers and a long tail.
What am I?

Georgia Bruce (6)
St Mary's Catholic Primary School, Bodmin

My First Riddle -
RIDDLES FROM ACROSS THE UK & OVERSEAS

A Riddle About A Cat

It is black and white.
It has four legs.
It has a medium head.
It has a tail that goes up.
It has whiskers and soft fur.
It lives in a house.
What is it?

Alex Hall-Walsh (6)
St Mary's Catholic Primary School, Bodmin

A Riddle About A Wildcat

I am spotty.
I have sharp teeth.
I have sharp claws.
I can run very fast.
I have a very long tail.
What am I?

Niall Harris (7)
St Mary's Catholic Primary School, Bodmin

A Riddle About A Bat

I have a red tongue.
I am smooth.
I come out and fly at night.
I have got long wings.
I sleep upside down.
You see lots of me on Halloween.
What am I?

Mya Barclay (6)
St Mary's Catholic Primary School, Bodmin

A Riddle About A Leopard

I live in Africa.
I have a long tail.
People want me for my skin.
I have sharp teeth to eat meat.
I have long claws.
I am golden with black and brown spots.
What am I?

Tegan Rowe (6)
St Mary's Catholic Primary School, Bodmin

Fairy Tale Riddle

I am nice.
I am gentle.
I am beautiful.
I went to the dwarves' cottage.
Who am I?
I am Snow White.

Daisy Church (5)
St Mary's CE Primary School, Writhlington

Fairy Tale Riddle

I am beautiful with brown hair.
I live in a castle.
I danced with a beast.
My friend is a clock.
Who am I?
Belle.

Aliyah Docherty (5)
St Mary's CE Primary School, Writhlington

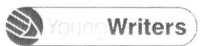

Fairy Tale Riddle

I am muscly.
I went up in the clouds.
I am scared.
Who am I?
I am Jack from 'Jack and the Beanstalk'.

Xavier Shipton (5)
St Mary's CE Primary School, Writhlington

Fairy Tale Riddle

We work underground.
We are small.
We found Snow White in our house.
Who are we?
We are the seven dwarves.

Alfie Padfield (6)
St Mary's CE Primary School, Writhlington

Fairy Tale Riddle

I am kind and work very hard
I used to wear rags
I lost my shoe at the ball
Who am I?
I am Cinderella.

Aaron Carver (6)
St Mary's CE Primary School, Writhlington

Fairy Tale Riddle

I wear a beautiful sparkly dress,
I do all the cleaning and cooking,
I have long blonde hair.
Who am I?
I am Cinderella.

Abi Bester (5)
St Mary's CE Primary School, Writhlington

Fairy Tale Riddle

I am beautiful with long blonde hair,
I am kind and gentle,
I have two ugly sisters.
Who am I?
I am Cinderella.

Emmi Myers (5)
St Mary's CE Primary School, Writhlington

Fairy Tale Riddle

I am beautiful and kind,
I went to the ball in a sparkly dress,
I used to wear old rags.
Who am I?
I am Cinderella.

Gracie Padfield (5)
St Mary's CE Primary School, Writhlington

My First Riddle -
RIDDLES FROM ACROSS THE UK & OVERSEAS

Fairy Tale Riddle

I smell of bleach.
I am energetic.
I went to the ball.
I lost my glass shoe.
Who am I?
I am Cinderella.

Lewis Harvey Davis (6)
St Mary's CE Primary School, Writhlington

Fairy Tale Riddle

I climb a beanstalk.
I get away from the giant.
I am kind and helpful.
Who am I?
I am Jack from 'Jack and the Beanstalk'.

Liam Williams (6)
St Mary's CE Primary School, Writhlington

What Am I?

I can fly anywhere.
I've got four long legs.
My favourite food is rotten fruit.
I sting to defend myself.
My family live in colonies.
My eggs hatch late in the summer.
What am I?
I am a wasp.

Antek Wozny (6)
Sandford School, Sandford

What Am I?

My legs are shiny and wiggly and there are six.
I live underground.
There are loads of us.
I eat honey, grubs and sweet things.
I am black.
I have three parts to my shiny body.
What am I?
I am an ant.

Ben Boughey (6)
Sandford School, Sandford

My First Riddle – RIDDLES FROM ACROSS THE UK & OVERSEAS

What Am I?

I am small but I can fly.
My wings are tiny.
You can't touch me because I will fly away.
I come out when it is sunny.
My friends and me are bright yellow with some black.
I do suck nectar.
What am I?
I am a bee.

Alice Board (7)
Sandford School, Sandford

My Toes

They are as big as the world,
They are as wriggly as jelly,
They are as round as a ball,
They are as soft as a pillow.
They are my toes.

Lucy Spiller (6)
Sidbury CE Primary School, Sidbury

My Head

It is as hard as rock,
It is as round as the world,
It is as brainy as a scientist,
It is as strong as a tree.
It is my head.

Luke Wheeler (6)
Sidbury CE Primary School, Sidbury

My Eyes

They are as round as the world,
They are sparkly like diamonds,
They are as small as mice,
They are gorgeous like a model's.
They are my eyes.

Maisie Lyon (6)
Sidbury CE Primary School, Sidbury

My First Riddle -
RIDDLES FROM ACROSS THE UK & OVERSEAS

My Toes

They are as smelly as socks,
They are as wriggly as worms,
They are as big as giants,
They are as bendy as caterpillars.
They are my toes.

Holly White (6)
Sidbury CE Primary School, Sidbury

My Teeth

They are as white as snow,
They are as wobbly as jelly,
They are as little as ants,
They are as clean as plates.
They are my teeth.

Sky Rowbotham (6)
Sidbury CE Primary School, Sidbury

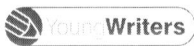

My Eyes

They are as sparkly as diamonds,
They are as round as a pizza,
They are as colourful as a rainbow,
They are as big as the world.
They are my eyes.

Alice Chapman (7)
Sidbury CE Primary School, Sidbury

My Elbows

They are as round as a roundabout,
They are as heavy as boulders,
They are knobbly as bones,
They are as pointy as sticks.
They are my elbows.

Oliver Beech (5)
Sidbury CE Primary School, Sidbury

My First Riddle –
RIDDLES FROM ACROSS THE UK & OVERSEAS

My Toes

They are as wriggly as worms,
They are as smelly as a skunk,
They are as small as teeth,
They are as bendy as bananas.
They are my toes.

William Bolton (5)
Sidbury CE Primary School, Sidbury

My Toes

They are as wriggly as worms,
They are as squiggly as an elephant's trunk,
They are as wobbly as jelly,
They are as jumpy as a grasshopper.
They are my toes.

George Chapman (5)
Sidbury CE Primary School, Sidbury

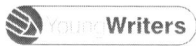

My Eyes

They are as sparkly as diamonds,
They are as bright as the sun,
They are as round as a roundabout,
They are as big as the world.
They are my eyes.

**Ben Green, Will Crick, Ben Fisher, Sam Putman,
Reuben Thomas (5) & Dylan Green (6)**
Sidbury CE Primary School, Sidbury

My Feet

They are as bendy as worms,
They are as stinky as toads,
They are as careful as a tortoise,
They are as big as the world.
They are my feet.

Freddie Eul-Barker (7)
Sidbury CE Primary School, Sidbury

My First Riddle –
RIDDLES FROM ACROSS THE UK & OVERSEAS

My Head

It is as strong as a horse,
It is as hot as fire,
It is as small as a ball,
It is as brainy as a scientist.
It is my head.

Jake White (6)
Sidbury CE Primary School, Sidbury

My Toes

They are as smelly as frogs,
They are as bendy as rubber,
They are as small as ants,
They are as wriggly as worms.
They are my toes.

Eve Chinery (6)
Sidbury CE Primary School, Sidbury

The Kangaroo And The Tiger

She has fur like a tiger.
She is beautiful like a baby.
She has a baby like a mummy.
She is bouncy like a rabbit.
She is orange like a tiger.
She is silent like a mouse.
She is handy like a horse.
She is ginormous like a robin.
She is fast like a lion.
She has floppy ears like a tiger.

Tayla Brazier
Stoneydelph Primary School, Stoneydelph

Stripy Zebra

She is fast like a cheetah
She is cute like a kitten
She is sweet like a puppy
She is fluffy like a butterfly
She is stripy like a tiger
She is a climber like a monkey
She is nice like a baby
She is lovely like a polar bear
She is cuddly like a teddy bear
She is white like a leopard.

Pheobe Brown (6)
Stoneydelph Primary School, Stoneydelph

My First Riddle – RIDDLES FROM ACROSS THE UK & OVERSEAS

Monkey

He is fast like a cheetah
He is cuddly like a teddy bear
He is huge like a gorilla
He is as big as a gorilla
He is jumpy like a cheetah
He is fluffy like a tiger.

Corey Drew (6)
Stoneydelph Primary School, Stoneydelph

The Little Brown Mouse

She is slow like a teddy bear.
She is smiley like a polar bear.
She is fast like a motorbike.
She is brown like a horse.
She has ears like a tiger.
She is funny like a donkey.
She is beautiful like a butterfly.
She is cheeky like a monkey.
She is fluffy like a bear.
She is tiny like a mouse.
She is pretty like a lady.
She is young like a baby.

Caitlin Riley
Stoneydelph Primary School, Stoneydelph

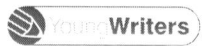

The Tiger

It is striped like a zebra.
It is fast like a fox.
It is smooth like an elephant.
It is long like a crocodile.
It is a tiger.

Jessica Harris-Powell (6)
Stoneydelph Primary School, Stoneydelph

The Lion

It is strong like a lion.
It is huge like an elephant.
It is fast like a cheetah.
It is scary like a vampire.

Korey Fulton (5)
Stoneydelph Primary School, Stoneydelph

My First Riddle - RIDDLES FROM ACROSS THE UK & OVERSEAS

The Giraffe

It is cuddly like a teddy.
It is stretchy like a rubber band.
It is spotty like a dog.
It has a long tail like a lion.
It is smooth like a cat.
It is high like a giant.
It is tall like a person.
It is a giraffe.

Quintana Jones
Stoneydelph Primary School, Stoneydelph

The Zebra

It is stripy like a tiger.
It is white and black.
It is famous like a queen bee.
It is fierce like a crocodile.

Megan Mellors
Stoneydelph Primary School, Stoneydelph

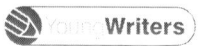

The Tiger

It is strong like a lion.
It is huge like a building.
It is fast like a cheetah.
It is scary like a vampire.

Dylan Dodwell (6)
Stoneydelph Primary School, Stoneydelph

Goal

It's as round as a sphere.
It's as blue as the sky.
It shoots off my trainers and goes really high,
Straight into the back of the net I bet!
My blue Everton football.

James Andrew Payton (7)
Ysgol Bryn Coch, Mold

My First Riddle –
RIDDLES FROM ACROSS THE UK & OVERSEAS

Magical Friend

She sits on my lap every day
She can run like a cheetah
She keeps me company
She plays with her toys like me and my brother
She is as black as a really dark night
She is Molly, our cat.

Callum Drew (6)
Ysgol Bryn Coch, Mold

A Riddle With A Not Very Nice Middle

It's in a fairy tale.
It bruises easily if it falls.
It can be put on a stick.
It was eaten by the Very Hungry Caterpillar on a Monday.
It can keep you healthy.
It is round, juicy and yummy.
It can be red or green.
It is an apple.

Melissa Hughes (7)
Ysgol Bryn Coch, Mold

Cotton Wool

I'm lots of different shapes and sizes.
I make you wet.
I move fast and slow.
I appear from nowhere.
I'm high in the sky.
When I'm down on the ground I'm foggy and misty.
I can hide the sun, moon and stars.
I'm Earth's blanket in the winter.
What am I?
I'm a cloud.

Josie Tattum (6)
Ysgol Bryn Coch, Mold

Who Am I?

I am as bright as a star.
I am as loveable as a teddy bear.
I am as nice as pie.
I am as good as gold.
I am as quiet as a mouse.
I am as happy as a clown.
I am me, Elliot!

Elliot Piers Lamb (6)
Ysgol Bryn Coch, Mold

My First Riddle –
RIDDLES FROM ACROSS THE UK & OVERSEAS

What Am I?

I can be hot
I can be cold
I get smelly
When I get old
I can come from a cow
Or even a goat
I get delivered to your door by a float
I go in coffee
I go in tea
What do you think I can be?

Jared Cresswell (6)
Ysgol Bryn Coch, Mold

My Animal Poem

He's black like the night but white like the snow
He's stripy like a tiger but with teeth like a horse
He can run like the wind on his hooves like a donkey
What is he?
He is a zebra of course.

Harry Stinton (7)
Ysgol Bryn Coch, Mold

Lazy Riddle

He has black spots,
He drinks a lot,
He likes to eat meat as a real treat,
Roar! Roar!
He's Charlie, the cheetah.

James Edwards (6)
Ysgol Bryn Coch, Mold

My Dad

He's as funny as a clown,
He's as clever as a teacher,
He's as happy as the sun,
He's as kind as a best friend,
He's as helpful as a policeman,
He is my dad and I love him.

Poppy May Evans (6)
Ysgol Bryn Coch, Mold

My First Riddle –
RIDDLES FROM ACROSS THE UK & OVERSEAS

My Kitten Disney

He is as small as a mouse
He is as fast as a cheetah
He claws like a lion
He eats like a gorilla
He is as bouncy as a trampoline
He is as cute as a baby
He is my kitten Disney.

Adam Stowell (6)
Ysgol Bryn Coch, Mold

The Tooth Fairy

I am very small and pretty
I visit you at night
I creep under your pillow
And take something small and white
I have a little present
It is a coin
I am your tooth fairy.

Grace Mair Brockley (6)
Ysgol Bryn Coch, Mold

Who Is He?

He's as playful as a puppy,
He's as loud as a roaring lion,
He's as sneaky as a snake,
He's as frisky as a ferret,
He's as smiley as a snappy crocodile,
He's as loveable as a little lamb,
But best of all, Mummy says he's just like me.
He's Arthur, my little brother.

Harry Crawshaw (7)
Ysgol Bryn Coch, Mold

Mousey

She's cute
She's pink
She's cuddly
She was a gift when I was born
She snuggles up with me at night
Although, she looks a little worn
She wears a bow upon her tail
Her belly's big and bouncy
I take her everywhere I go
She is, my favourite Mousey!

Ella Blythin (6)
Ysgol Bryn Coch, Mold

My First Riddle – RIDDLES FROM ACROSS THE UK & OVERSEAS

The Dolphin

It can swim like a fish.
It can jump higher than a kangaroo.
It is always smiling everywhere.
It looks like a mermaid.
It is cuter than a puppy.
It is kinder than a shark.
It is a dolphin.

Katie Lenden (6)
Ysgol Bryn Coch, Mold

The Red Squirrel In The Tree

Our colour is red
Our cousins are grey
Our tails are bushy
Our nest is a drey
We like to eat nuts
And climb in the tree
You won't see us very often
What are we?

Lauren Hannah Cox (6)
Ysgol Bryn Coch, Mold

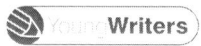

My Favourite Place

My name is Charlie Cooper.
I ride there on my scooter.
It's not far from my house.
Sometimes it's quiet as a mouse.
I go there in the day
To have a little play
Even in the dark.
My favourite place is . . . the park.

Charlie Cooper (6)
Ysgol Bryn Coch, Mold

The Moon

Sometimes I am full
Sometimes I am half
I sleep all day
You can only see my funny face when it is dark
People talk of aliens on me
My friends are the stars
In the day I am hidden
I light up the sky at night
Look up at me
I am the man in the moon.

Deran Hughes (6)
Ysgol Bryn Coch, Mold

My First Riddle - RIDDLES FROM ACROSS THE UK & OVERSEAS

The Plane

Sometimes I am big
Sometimes I am small
I have wings and a coloured tail
I love to take off
Then land in hot places
I fly down the runway
And people have smiles on their faces
I am a plane.

Kaelum Hughes (6)
Ysgol Bryn Coch, Mold

My Name

My first is in orange, but never in rage.
My second is in lie and also in fly.
My third is half of a useful pair,
But only in sound, not written, so there!
My fourth is in five and also in hive.
My fifth is in dance, so let's have a jive.
My last is in riddle and also in crime.
So I hope you can find me hidden deep in this rhyme.
Answer: Oliver.

Oliver Cheatle (6)
Ysgol Bryn Coch, Mold

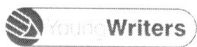

Volcano

Their rumbles are very loud.
They can make their own cloud.
They create land with their power
With a molten rock shower.
Nothing puts on a better firework show
Than a . . . volcano!

Joel Eccles (6)
Ysgol Bryn Coch, Mold

My First Riddle -
RIDDLES FROM ACROSS THE UK & OVERSEAS

Young Writers Information

We hope you have enjoyed reading this book - and that you will continue to enjoy it in the coming years.
If you like reading and writing poetry drop us a line, or give us a call, and we'll send you a free information pack.
Alternatively if you would like to order further copies of this book or any of our other titles, then please give us a call or log onto our website at www.youngwriters.co.uk.

Young Writers Information
Remus House
Coltsfoot Drive
Peterborough
PE2 9BF
(01733) 890066